DOT-TO-DOT
ANIMALS

Karen Bryant-Mole

Illustrated By Graham Round

Edited by Jenny Tyler

Cat and mouse set off

1 2 3 4 5 6 7 8 9 10 11 12 13 14 15 16 17 18 19 20 21 22 23 24 25 26

Cat and mouse are going on an expedition to see how many different animals they can find.

- Join the red and blue dots to find out how they are travelling.

- Join the yellow dots to see what spider is doing.

In the rainforest

Cat and mouse have landed in the hot, steamy rainforest.

- Join the red dots to find a rainforest bird.

- Do you know what the largest kind of ape is called?
  Join the blue dots to find one.

1 2 3 4 5 6 7 8 9 10 11 12 13 14 15 16 17 18 19 20 21 22 23 24 25 26

- Join the green dots to find out which animal is hiding in the grass.

- Join the yellow dots to find another animal. What is it?

- Can you find another animal with stripes?

In the garden

Cat and mouse have flown in to help with the gardening.

- Join the blue dots to see an animal which started life as a caterpillar.

1 2 3 4 5 6 7 8 9 10 11 12 13 14 15 16 17 18 19 20 21 22 23 24 25 26

- Join the yellow, green and brown dots.

- Which animal has eight feet? Which animal has no feet?
  Which animal has one foot?

Underwater adventure

Cat and mouse are exploring underwater in a submarine.

- Join the red dots to see what it looks like.
- Which undersea animal has eight legs?
  Join the yellow dots to find out.

1 2 3 4 5 6 7 8 9 10 11 12 13 14 15 16 17 18 19 20 21 22 23 24 25 26

- Join the blue dots to find a dolphin.
- Find two more undersea animals by joining the green and orange dots. What are they?

On safari

Cat and mouse are on safari in the grasslands of Africa.

- Join the green and red dots to see what they are travelling in.

1 2 3 4 5 6 7 8 9 10 11 12 13 14 15 16 17 18 19 20 21 22 23 24 25 26

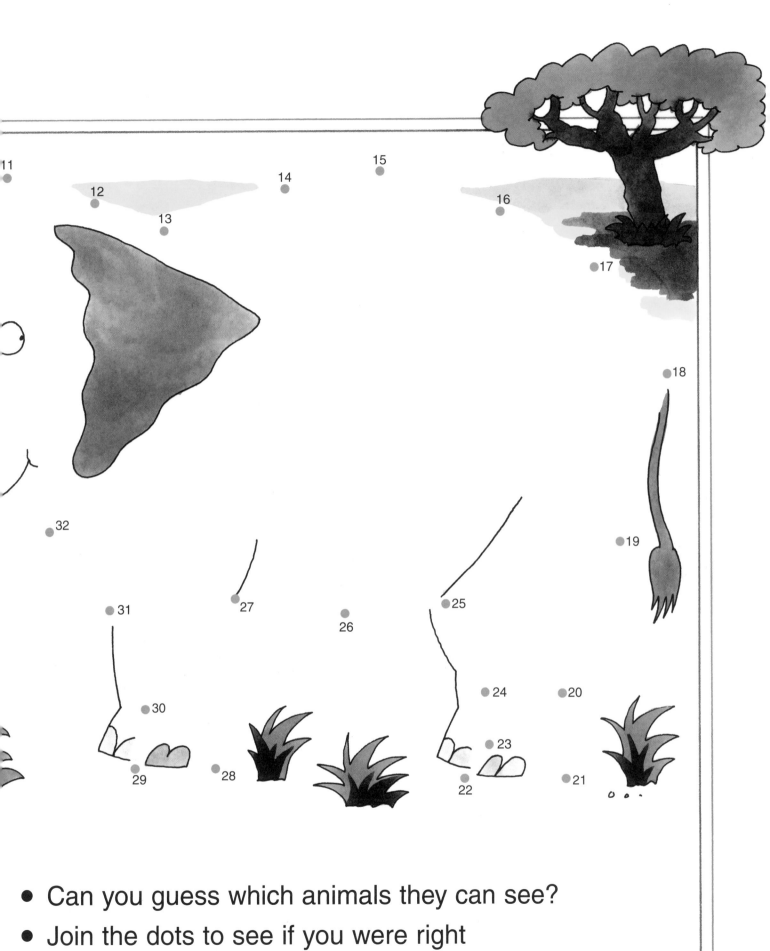

11

12

13

14

15

16

17

18

19

32

31

30

29

28

27

26

25

24

23

22

21

20

- Can you guess which animals they can see?
- Join the dots to see if you were right

28 29 30 31 32 33 34 35 36 37 38 39 40 41 42 43 44 45 46 47 48 49 50

At the seaside

- Cat has been busy.
  Join the yellow dots to find out what he has been doing.
- Join the pink dots to discover why mouse has dropped his ice cream.

1 2 3 4 5 6 7 8 9 10 11 12 13 14 15 16 17 18 19 20 21 22 23 24 25 26

- Where is frog? Join the red dots to find out.
- What can you see if you join the blue dots?
- Join the orange dots to find out what is lying on the beach.

28 29 30 31 32 33 34 35 36 37 38 39 40 41 42 43 44 45 46 47 48 49 50

Under the ground

Cat and mouse are investigating life under the ground.

- Mouse has found an animal whose home is called a set.

- Join the blue dots to find out what it is.

- Join the green dots to find its set.

1 2 3 4 5 6 7 8 9 10 11 12 13 14 15 16 17 18 19 20 21 22 23 24 25 26

- Which animal lives in a den? Join the brown dots to find out.
- Join the orange dots to see its den.
- There are two more animals to find.
  Join the dots to see what they are.

By the river

- Join the orange dots to find an otter.
- Otters live in river banks.
  Join the green dots to see the edge of this river bank.
- Join the yellow dots. What can you see?

1 2 3 4 5 6 7 8 9 10 11 12 13 14 15 16 17 18 19 20 21 22 23 24 25 26

- Do you know what a kingfisher looks like? Join the blue dots to find out.

- When you join the red dots you will find something with two sets of wings. Do you know what it is called?

At the farm

Cat and mouse are visiting a farm.

- What is cat doing? Join the blue dots to help you to see.
- Who is hiding inside the henhouse?

- What is mouse doing? Join the brown dots to find out.
- Join the other dots to find some more farm animals.

An icy expedition

Cat and mouse have arrived in the frozen North.

- Join the red dots to see how they got there.
- Join the blue dots to see where they will stay.
- Who is cat playing snowballs with? Join the yellow dots to se

1 2 3 4 5 6 7 8 9 10 11 12 13 14 15 16 17 18 19 20 21 22 23 24 25 26

- What is mouse doing?
  Join the green dots to find out.

- Join the orange and brown dots to find two more
  animals that live in cold places. What are they?

In the forest

Cat and mouse are walking through the forest.

- Join the red dots to see something they must not touch.

- Join the pink and green dots to find two woodland birds.

- Join the blue dots to see spider's home.

1 2 3 4 5 6 7 8 9 10 11 12 13 14 15 16 17 18 19 20 21 22 23 24 25 26

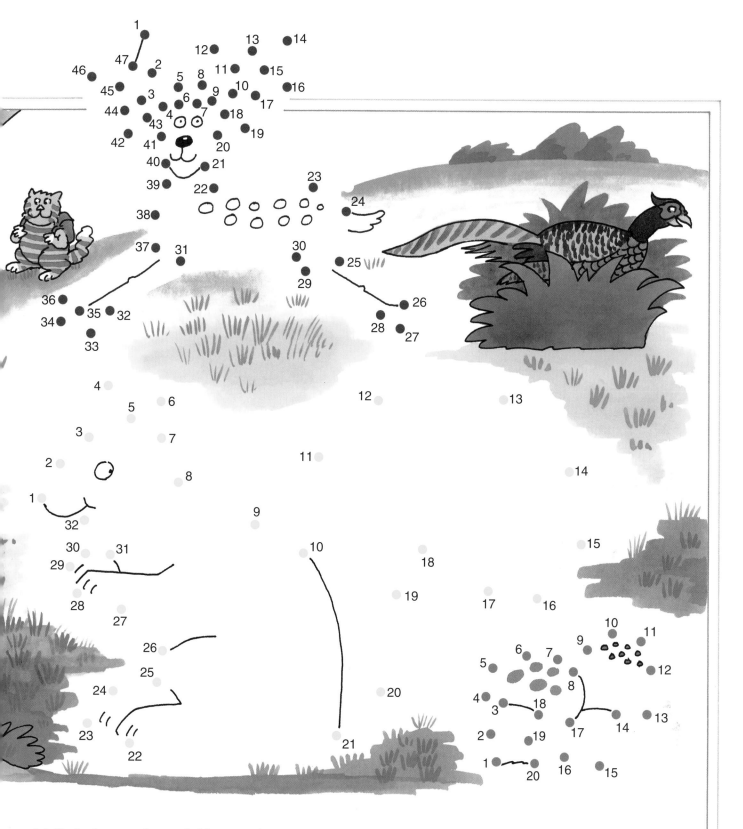

- Which animal lives in trees and eats nuts?
  Join the yellow dots to find out.

- Join the brown dots to see an animal whose babies
  are called fawns.

Home again

Cat and mouse are coming home after their exciting expedition.

- What is mouse pushing? Join the dots to see.

- Can you see how many suitcases they have brought with them?